THE AUSTRALIAN
Women's Weekly
cooking in 10,20,30 minutes

acp
books

contents

The oven temperatures in this book are for conventional ovens; if you have a fan-forced oven, decrease the temperature by 10-20 degrees. A measurement conversion chart appears on the back flap of this book.

shortcuts

Preparing delicious weeknight meals in less than 30 minutes is not as challenging as it sounds. In fact, with these helpful shopping tips, a few cooking shortcuts and our simple fresh recipes, it's easy. Enjoy spending less time in the kitchen after work and more time around the table with your family.

SHOPPING

PLAN AHEAD

A well-designed weekly meal plan means fewer trips to the supermarket. Work out a plan including breakfasts, lunches, dinners and snacks/treats for the entire week. Schedule quick and simple weekday meals when you may be time-poor and leave more complex recipes for the weekend. The time spent developing the meal plan will be well worth it when you no longer have to fret over what to make for dinner tonight.

MAKE A LIST

Make a shopping list of exactly what you need for your meal plan and stick to it. Don't buy anything that's not on the list and that you have no plan to use. Try to group items according to aisles, such as fresh produce; dairy; dry store (oil, flour, sugar, pasta and rice); bakery; freezer and so on. You will soon be navigating the aisles with ease.

PACK THE PANTRY

Keep your pantry stocked with staples and you won't be caught out when you come to prepare dinner. Tetra packs of stock; plain and self-raising flour; sugar; olive oil; pasta and rice; canned fruits, tomatoes, salmon and tuna; canned and dried beans and lentils; bottled sauces, pastes, dressings and condiments are all commonly used ingredients and there's no hurry to use them up. Keep an eye out for "specials" on non-perishables and buy them in bulk. Always have eggs, butter and cheese in your refrigerator and have ready-rolled sheets of puff and shortcrust pastry in the freezer.

COOKING

LEFTOVERS

Make larger quantities of dinners and pack the leftovers for lunch the next day. Or find a few recipes that make two meals from one – leftover beef stew can easily become a pie with a pastry or mashed potato top; leftover bolognese becomes chilli con carne with some added chilli flakes and a can of beans or use as a taco filling with salsa, shredded lettuce and sour cream.

FREEZING

Use your weekends wisely and make big batches of soups, stews and curries that freeze well. Label, date and freeze individual or meal-sized servings in plastic containers. Thawing a homemade curry on a weeknight, when you have nothing left in the pantry, is more of a treat and far less expensive than takeaway.

CONVENIENCE

Take advantage of partially pre-prepared meats sold at your butcher. There are a whole range of trimmed, marinated, crumbed, skewered, sliced and diced meats available to help you cut cooking times. Find a fishmonger that sells partially prepared seafood – shelled and deveined prawns, cleaned squid hoods, boneless fish fillets and marinara mix – seafood is a healthy meal option for your family and takes almost no time to cook once the hard work has been done for you.

10 minute
mains

prawn and pesto linguine

375g (12 ounces) linguine pasta

2 cloves garlic

1 fresh long red chilli

2 medium zucchini (240g)

500g (1 pound) shelled uncooked large king prawns (shrimp), tails intact

180g (6 ounces) bottled chunky basil pesto dip

1 Cook pasta in large saucepan of boiling water until tender; drain, reserving ⅓ cup cooking liquid. Return pasta to pan.

2 Meanwhile, crush garlic. Thinly slice chilli. Peel zucchini lengthways into ribbons.

3 Heat oiled large frying pan; cook prawns until changed in colour. Add garlic, chilli and zucchini to pan; cook, stirring, until zucchini softens.

4 Add pesto, prawn mixture and reserved cooking liquid to pasta; toss gently, season to taste.

prep + cook time **10 minutes**
serves **4**
nutritional count per serving
20.9g total fat
(4.4g saturated fat); 2633kJ
(630 cal); 65.7g carbohydrate;
41.5g protein; 5.4g fibre

thai green prawn curry

2 tablespoons green curry paste

500g (1 pound) shelled uncooked medium king prawns (shrimp), tails intact

2 teaspoons fish sauce

1⅔ cups (410ml) coconut milk

½ cup (125ml) water

150g (4½ ounces) snow peas

500g (1 pound) gai lan

¼ cup loosely packed fresh thai basil leaves

1 Cook curry paste in heated large deep frying pan, stirring, until fragrant.

2 Add prawns, sauce, coconut milk and the water to pan; bring to the boil, stirring. Reduce heat; simmer, uncovered, 3 minutes.

3 Meanwhile, trim and halve snow peas. Cut gai lan into 5cm (2-inch) lengths.

4 Add vegetables to pan; simmer, uncovered, about 2 minutes or until prawns change colour and sauce thickens. Season to taste.

5 Serve curry sprinkled with thai basil.

prep + cook time 10 minutes
serves 4
nutritional count per serving
25.4g total fat
(18.6g saturated fat); 1639kJ
(392 cal); 7.8g carbohydrate;
30.9g protein; 5.4g fibre

serving suggestion Serve with steamed jasmine rice.

peri peri fish with herb salad

peri peri fish with herb salad

4 x 200g (6½-ounce) firm white fish fillets

⅓ cup (80ml) peri peri marinade

80g (2½ ounces) baby rocket (arugula) leaves

⅓ cup firmly packed fresh mint leaves

¼ cup firmly packed fresh flat-leaf parsley leaves

1 tablespoon lemon juice

1 Drizzle fish with marinade, coating both sides. Cook fish in heated oiled large frying pan.
2 Meanwhile, combine rocket, mint, parsley and juice in medium bowl; season to taste.
3 Serve fish with salad.

prep + cook time 10 minutes
serves 4
nutritional count per serving
5.1g total fat
(1.5g saturated fat); 991kJ
(237 cal); 4.7g carbohydrate;
41.7g protein; 1.7g fibre

tips We used blue-eye in this recipe, but any white fish fillet will be fine. Peri peri, or piri piri, is a hot chilli sauce used in African, Portuguese and Brazilian cookery. It is available from gourmet food stores and most major supermarkets.

garlic and chilli mussels

garlic and chilli mussels

60g (2 ounces) butter

3 cloves garlic

1 fresh long red chilli

⅓ cup (80ml) dry white wine

1kg (2 pounds) cleaned small black mussels

⅓ cup coarsely chopped fresh flat-leaf parsley

1 Chop butter coarsely. Heat butter in large saucepan until melted.
2 Meanwhile, finely chop garlic and slice chilli. Add garlic and chilli to pan, cook, stirring, until fragrant. Add wine; bring to the boil.
3 Add mussels to pan; simmer, covered, until mussels open. Stir in parsley; season to taste.

prep + cook time 10 minutes
serves 4
nutritional count per serving
13.3g total fat
(8.4g saturated fat); 702kJ
(168 cal); 2.8g carbohydrate;
6.3g protein; 0.6g fibre

tip To save time, buy pre-cleaned, bearded mussels.
serving suggestion Serve with crusty bread to mop up the juices.

garlicky lemon chicken

6 chicken thigh fillets (1.2kg)

3 cloves garlic

1 medium lemon (140g)

2 tablespoons coarsely chopped fresh flat-leaf parsley

1 tablespoon water

1 Halve chicken fillets. Cook chicken in heated oiled large frying pan.
2 Meanwhile, crush garlic. Finely grate 2 teaspoons rind from lemon. Squeeze 2 tablespoons juice from lemon.
3 Add garlic, rind, juice, parsley and the water to pan. Turn chicken to coat; season to taste.

prep + cook time 10 minutes
serves 4
nutritional count per serving
21.7g total fat
(6.6g saturated fat); 1760kJ
(421 cal); 0.6g carbohydrate;
56.1g protein; 0.6g fibre

serving suggestion Serve with mixed salad leaves or steamed green beans.

teriyaki salmon

4 x 220g (7-ounce) salmon
fillets, skin on

2 tablespoons japanese
soy sauce

2 tablespoons mirin

2 tablespoons water

1 tablespoon light brown sugar

1 green onion (scallion)

1 Heat oiled large frying pan;
cook salmon, skin-side down,
about 5 minutes or until skin is
crisp. Turn salmon; add sauce to
pan with mirin, the water and
sugar; simmer, uncovered, until
salmon is cooked as desired.
2 Meanwhile, thinly slice onion.
3 Serve salmon drizzled with pan
juices; sprinkle with onion.

prep + cook time 10 minutes
serves 4
nutritional count per serving
15.6g total fat
(3.5g saturated fat); 1404kJ
(336 cal); 3.8g carbohydrate;
43.5g protein; 0.1g fibre

serving suggestion Serve with
steamed asian greens.

moroccan chicken with couscous

12 chicken tenderloins (900g)

2 tablespoons
moroccan seasoning

1¼ cups (250g) couscous

1¼ cups (310ml) boiling water

⅓ cup (45g) slivered almonds

⅓ cup (55g) sultanas

½ cup coarsely chopped fresh
coriander (cilantro)

½ cup (140g) yogurt

1 Sprinkle chicken with seasoning; cook in heated oiled large frying pan.
2 Meanwhile, combine couscous with the water in large heatproof bowl, cover; stand about 5 minutes or until water is absorbed, fluffing with fork occasionally.
3 Roast nuts in small frying pan until browned lightly.
4 Stir nuts, sultanas and coriander into couscous; season to taste.
5 Divide couscous into serving bowls; top with chicken and yogurt.

prep + cook time 10 minutes
serves 4
nutritional count per serving
13g total fat
(2.6g saturated fat); 2600kJ
(622 cal); 60.4g carbohydrate;
63.3g protein; 2.5g fibre

Veal schnitzel is thinly sliced steak available crumbed or plain (uncrumbed); we used plain schnitzel, also called escalopes, in this recipe.

veal with caper, lemon and butter sauce

6 thin veal schnitzels (600g)

1 tablespoon cracked black pepper

60g (2 ounces) butter

1 tablespoon drained baby capers

2 medium lemons (280g)

1 tablespoon water

⅓ cup coarsely chopped fresh flat-leaf parsley

1 Cut veal in half. Sprinkle pepper on both sides of veal. Heat butter in large frying pan; cook veal, in batches, until browned lightly on both sides. Remove from pan; cover to keep warm.

2 Meanwhile, place capers in small sieve, rinse. Remove rind from half of one lemon with zester. Squeeze ⅓ cup juice from lemons.

3 Add capers, zest, juice and the water to pan; bring to the boil, stirring. Season to taste.

4 Transfer veal to serving plates. Spoon sauce over veal; sprinkle with parsley.

prep + cook time 10 minutes
serves 4
nutritional count per serving
14.6g total fat
(8.7g saturated fat); 1137kJ
(272 cal); 1.1g carbohydrate;
33.8g protein; 0.4g fibre

grilled lamb chops with tomato and olive salsa

grilled lamb chops with tomato and olive salsa

¼ cup loosely packed fresh oregano leaves

8 lamb loin chops (800g)

250g (8 ounces) cherry tomatoes

½ cup (75g) seeded kalamata olives

2 tablespoons french dressing

100g (3 ounces) rocket (arugula)

1 Finely chop half the oregano; combine with chops in large bowl.
2 Season chops; cook on heated oiled grill plate (or grill or barbecue).
3 Meanwhile, to make tomato and olive salsa, quarter tomatoes; halve olives. Combine tomato, olives, dressing and remaining oregano in medium bowl. Season to taste.
4 Serve chops with salsa and rocket.

prep + cook time 10 minutes
serves 4
nutritional count per serving
16.2g total fat
(6.6g saturated fat); 1333kJ
(319 cal); 8.2g carbohydrate;
33.9g protein; 2.2g fibre

dukkah lamb cutlets with honey

dukkah lamb cutlets with honey

12 french-trimmed lamb cutlets (600g)

¼ cup (30g) dukkah spice mix

2 tablespoons honey

2 tablespoons pomegranate molasses

1 Dip both sides of lamb cutlets into dukkah mix.
2 Cook cutlets, in batches, in heated oiled large frying pan.
3 Serve cutlets drizzled with combined honey and molasses.

prep + cook time 10 minutes
serves 4
nutritional count per serving
11.5g total fat
(3g saturated fat); 941kJ
(225 cal); 13.5g carbohydrate;
17g protein; 1.4g fibre

tip Pomegranate molasses has a tart, fruity taste similar to balsamic vinegar. It is available at Middle Eastern food stores and specialty food shops.
serving suggestion Serve with herbed couscous.

smoky beans with chorizo

1 large red onion (300g)

1 large red capsicum
(bell pepper) (350g)

1 cured chorizo sausage (170g)

2 teaspoons smoked paprika

800g (1½ pounds) canned
borlotti beans

800g (1½ pounds) canned
crushed tomatoes

2 tablespoons coarsely chopped
fresh flat-leaf parsley

1 Peel and coarsely chop
onion. Coarsely chop capsicum
and chorizo.
2 Heat oiled large saucepan;
cook onion, capsicum and
chorizo, stirring, until vegetables
are tender. Add paprika; cook,
stirring, until fragrant.
3 Meanwhile, rinse and drain
beans. Add beans and undrained
tomatoes to pan; bring to the
boil. Reduce heat; simmer,
uncovered, about 5 minutes or
until sauce has thickened slightly.
Season to taste.
4 Serve sprinkled with parsley.

prep + cook time 10 minutes
serves 6
nutritional count per serving
9.4g total fat
(3.3g saturated fat); 1225kJ
(293 cal); 33g carbohydrate;
15.9g protein; 6.2g fibre

serving suggestion Serve with
crusty white bread.

honey mustard lamb cutlets

1 tablespoon dijon mustard

1 tablespoon
wholegrain mustard

2 tablespoons honey

1 tablespoon white
wine vinegar

12 french-trimmed lamb
cutlets (600g)

400g (12½ ounces) green beans

1 Combine mustards, honey and vinegar in a small jug. Combine half the honey mixture with lamb cutlets in large bowl.

2 Cook cutlets in heated oiled large frying pan.

3 Meanwhile, trim beans. Boil, steam or microwave beans until tender; drain.

4 Serve cutlets with green beans; drizzle with remaining honey mixture.

prep + cook time 10 minutes
serves 4
nutritional count per serving
13.2g total fat
(5.9g saturated fat); 1058kJ
(253 cal); 4.5g carbohydrate;
17.7g protein; 2.9g fibre

Try using a variety of mushrooms such as button, flat, cup and portobello.

creamy mushroom and spinach gnocchi

625g (1¼ pounds) fresh potato gnocchi

375g (12 ounces) assorted mushrooms

2 cloves garlic

1¼ cups (300ml) pouring cream

90g (3 ounces) baby spinach leaves

⅓ cup (25g) finely grated parmesan cheese

1 Cook gnocchi in large saucepan of boiling water until tender; drain.

2 Meanwhile, thinly slice mushrooms. Crush garlic.

3 Cook mushrooms and garlic in heated oiled large frying pan, stirring, until softened. Add cream and spinach; bring to the boil. Reduce heat, simmer, uncovered, until spinach wilts and sauce thickens. Stir in half the cheese. Season to taste.

4 Add gnocchi to pan, stir gently. Serve gnocchi topped with remaining cheese.

prep + cook time 10 minutes
serves 4
nutritional count per serving
36.2g total fat
(23.4g saturated fat); 2458kJ
(588 cal); 48.2g carbohydrate;
14.4g protein; 6.8g fibre

Pappardelle are flat, wide pasta ribbons – sometimes they have scalloped edges. Tagliatelle or fettuccine can be substituted.

pappardelle carbonara

8 slices prosciutto (120g)

375g (12 ounces) pappardelle pasta

3 eggs

½ cup (125ml) pouring cream

½ cup (40g) finely grated parmesan cheese

¼ cup coarsely chopped fresh flat-leaf parsley

1 Thinly slice prosciutto. Cook prosciutto in heated oiled large frying pan until crisp; remove from pan.
2 Cook pasta in large saucepan of boiling water until tender; drain, reserving ½ cup cooking liquid. Return pasta to pan over low heat.
3 Meanwhile, lightly beat eggs, cream and cheese in large jug.
4 Add egg mixture, reserved cooking liquid, half the parsley and half the prosciutto to pasta. Toss gently, season to taste.
5 Serve pasta topped with remaining prosciutto and parsley.

prep + cook time 10 minutes
serves 4
nutritional count per serving
22.6g total fat
(12.7g saturated fat); 2349kJ
(562 cal); 65g carbohydrate;
22.7g protein; 3.3g fibre

10 minute sides

cucumber and fetta salad with za'atar

2 lebanese cucumbers (260g)

90g (3 ounces) goat's milk fetta cheese

2 tablespoons finely chopped fresh mint

1 tablespoon lemon juice

1 tablespoon olive oil

2 teaspoons za'atar

1 Peel cucumbers and slice thinly. Arrange cucumber on large serving platter.
2 Combine crumbled fetta and mint in small bowl; sprinkle mixture over cucumber.
3 Drizzle salad with juice and oil, then sprinkle with za'atar. Season to taste.

prep time 10 minutes **serves** 4
nutritional count per serving
9.9g total fat
(4.1g saturated fat); 468kJ
(112 cal); 1.2g carbohydrate;
4.3g protein; 0.7g fibre

tip Za'atar is a Middle Eastern blend of whole roasted sesame seeds, sumac and crushed dried herbs such as wild marjoram and thyme, although its content is largely determined by the individual maker. It is available from some large supermarkets, delicatessens and Middle Eastern food stores. Replace it with dried oregano if unavailable.

spinach couscous

1½ cups (300g) couscous

1½ cups (375ml) boiling water

60g (2 ounces) baby
spinach leaves

2 green onions (scallions)

1 Combine couscous with the
water in large heatproof bowl.
Cover; stand 5 minutes or until
water is absorbed, fluffing with
fork occasionally.
2 Shred spinach finely. Slice
onions thinly. Stir spinach and
onion into couscous; season
to taste.

prep time 10 minutes **serves** 6
nutritional count per serving
0.3g total fat
(0.1g saturated fat); 786kJ
(188 cal); 38.5g carbohydrate;
6.7g protein; 0.8g fibre

tomato and herb salad

5 medium tomatoes (750g)

¼ cup coarsely chopped fresh flat-leaf parsley

2 tablespoons each coarsely chopped fresh mint and dill

2 cloves garlic

2 tablespoons lemon juice

1 tablespoon olive oil

2 teaspoons white vinegar

1 Chop tomatoes coarsely. Place tomatoes and herbs in medium bowl.
2 Crush garlic. Place garlic, juice, oil and vinegar in screw-top jar; season to taste, shake well.
3 Drizzle dressing over salad; toss gently to combine.

prep time 10 minutes **serves** 6
nutritional count per serving
3.2g total fat
(0.4g saturated fat); 213kJ
(51 cal); 2.7g carbohydrate;
1.5g protein; 1.9g fibre

tomato and preserved lemon salad

750g (1½ pounds) baby roma (egg) truss tomatoes

1 small red onion (100g)

½ cup firmly packed fresh coriander (cilantro) leaves

preserved lemon dressing

1 wedge preserved lemon

1 clove garlic

⅓ cup (80ml) lemon juice

2 tablespoons olive oil

1 tablespoon finely chopped fresh flat-leaf parsley

½ teaspoon white (granulated) sugar

¼ teaspoon ground cumin

pinch sweet paprika

1 Make preserved lemon dressing.

2 Halve tomatoes. Slice onion thinly. Combine tomato, onion, coriander and dressing in large bowl; season to taste.

PRESERVED LEMON DRESSING
Discard flesh from preserved lemon, wash and dry rind; slice thinly. Crush garlic. Place rind and garlic with remaining ingredients in screw-top jar; shake well.

prep time 10 minutes **serves** 6
nutritional count per serving
6.3g total fat
(0.9g saturated fat); 355kJ
(85 cal); 4.5g carbohydrate;
1g protein; 2.4g fibre

beetroot and fetta salad

beetroot and fetta salad

440g (14 ounces) canned whole baby beetroot (beets)

100g (3 ounces) mesclun

1 cup firmly packed fresh mint leaves

250g (8 ounces) bottled marinated fetta cheese in oil

1 teaspoon balsamic vinegar

1 teaspoon dijon mustard

1 Drain and halve beetroot. Divide beetroot, mesclun and mint between serving bowls.
2 Drain cheese, reserving 2 tablespoons of oil. Chop cheese into cubes, divide between serving bowls.
3 Combine reserved oil with vinegar and mustard in small bowl; season to taste, drizzle over salad.

prep time 10 minutes **serves** 6
nutritional count per serving
13.1g total fat
(5.3g saturated fat); 694kJ
(166 cal); 5.3g carbohydrate;
6.4g protein; 2.3g fibre

broccolini with honey

broccolini with honey

700g (1½ pounds) broccolini

2 teaspoons sesame seeds

1 tablespoon light soy sauce

1 tablespoon boiling water

2 teaspoons honey

1 Halve broccolini crossways. Cook broccolini in large baking paper-lined steamer, over large saucepan of simmering water, about 5 minutes or until tender.
2 Meanwhile, toast sesame seeds in a small dry frying pan until browned lightly.
3 Combine sauce, the water and honey in small jug; season to taste.
4 Serve broccolini drizzled with sauce and sprinkled with sesame seeds.

prep + cook time 10 minutes
serves 4
nutritional count per serving
1.3g total fat
(0g saturated fat); 326kJ
(78 cal); 4.1g carbohydrate;
8.8g protein; 7.3g fibre

warm balsamic mushroom salad

warm balsamic mushroom salad

8 slices pancetta (120g)

½ cup (125ml) balsamic italian dressing

⅓ cup (80ml) water

500g (1 pound) small button mushrooms

1 teaspoon fresh thyme leaves

90g (3 ounces) mixed salad leaves

90g (3 ounces) fetta cheese

1 Cook pancetta in heated oiled large frying pan until crisp. When cool enough to handle, break into large pieces.
2 Heat dressing and the water in same frying pan; cook mushrooms and thyme, stirring, until mushrooms are tender and liquid has almost evaporated. Season to taste.
3 Place mushrooms and pancetta in large bowl with salad leaves; toss gently to combine.
4 Serve salad sprinkled with crumbled fetta.

prep + cook time 10 minutes
serves 4
nutritional count per serving
19.9g total fat
(6g saturated fat); 1066kJ
(255 cal); 3.1g carbohydrate;
14.6g protein; 3.8g fibre

garlic bread

garlic bread

1 loaf turkish bread (430g)

50g (1½ ounces) butter

2 cloves garlic

2 tablespoons finely chopped fresh flat-leaf parsley

1 Halve bread horizontally; cut each half into four pieces.
2 Heat butter in small saucepan until melted. Crush garlic. Add garlic to butter with parsley; brush over cut sides of bread pieces.
3 Cook bread on heated oiled grill plate (or grill or barbecue) until browned both sides.

prep + cook time 10 minutes
serves 4
nutritional count per serving
11.2g total fat
(5.9g saturated fat); 1229kJ
(294 cal); 38.9g carbohydrate;
7.9g protein; 2.6g fibre

20 minute mains

rocket, chilli and lemon spaghetti

375g (12 ounces) spaghetti

1 fresh long red chilli

1 clove garlic

150g (4½ ounces) baby rocket
(arugula) leaves

⅓ cup (80ml) lemon-infused
olive oil

1 cup (80g) finely grated
parmesan cheese

1 medium lemon (140g)

1 Cook pasta in large saucepan
of boiling water until tender;
drain, reserving ⅓ cup (80ml) of
the cooking liquid.
2 Meanwhile, finely chop chilli.
Crush garlic. Chop rocket coarsely.
3 Combine oil, chilli and garlic
in small frying pan; heat gently,
about 5 minutes or until hot
and fragrant.
4 Return pasta to pan with the
chilli oil, reserved cooking liquid
and rocket; toss gently to
combine. Season to taste.
5 Cut lemon into wedges.
Serve pasta with cheese and
lemon wedges.

prep + cook time 15 minutes
serves 4
nutritional count per serving
19.4g total fat
(2.8g saturated fat); 2031kJ
(486 cal); 64.6g carbohydrate;
11.2g protein; 3.6g fibre

tip Garlic-infused olive oil
can be used instead of the
lemon-infused oil in this recipe.

belgian mussels

3 medium tomatoes (450g)

2 cloves garlic

1½ cups (375ml) beer

¼ cup (60ml) sweet chilli sauce

1kg (2 pounds) cleaned small black mussels

¼ cup coarsely chopped fresh flat-leaf parsley

1 Coarsely chop tomatoes; thinly slice garlic. Bring tomato, garlic, beer and sauce to the boil in large saucepan. Reduce heat; simmer, uncovered, about 5 minutes or until tomato is soft.
2 Add mussels to pan; cook, covered, about 5 minutes or until mussels open. Season to taste.
3 Serve mussels with sauce and sprinkled with parsley.

prep + cook time 15 minutes
serves 4
nutritional count per serving
1.5g total fat
(0.4g saturated fat); 481kJ
(115 cal); 9.4g carbohydrate;
7.8g protein; 2.5g fibre

tip To save time, buy pre-cleaned, bearded mussels.
serving suggestion Serve with crusty bread to mop up the juices.

veal with lemon and oregano

2 cloves garlic

2 medium (280g) lemons

¼ cup (60ml) olive oil

¼ cup loosely packed fresh oregano leaves

8 x 100g (3-ounce) thin veal schnitzels

2 teaspoons finely chopped fresh flat-leaf parsley

1 Thinly slice garlic. Finely grate 1 teaspoon rind from lemon. Squeeze ⅔ cup juice from lemons.
2 Heat half the oil in large frying pan; cook garlic and oregano, stirring, until garlic is fragrant and oregano is crisp. Remove with a slotted spoon; drain on absorbent paper.
3 Add remaining oil to pan; cook veal, in batches, until browned both sides. Add rind, juice and parsley to pan; cook 1 minute.
4 Serve veal drizzled with pan juices; sprinkle with garlic and oregano mixture. Season to taste.

prep + cook time 15 minutes
serves 4
nutritional count per serving
21.3g total fat
(3.4g saturated fat); 1576kJ
(377 cal); 1.3g carbohydrate;
45g protein; 0.4g fibre

tip Veal schnitzel is thinly sliced steak available crumbed or plain (uncrumbed); we used plain schnitzel, also called escalopes, in this recipe.
serving suggestion Serve with mixed salad leaves.

Pepato is an Italian sheep's milk cheese, most often pecorino, studded with peppercorns. It is available from some delicatessens and specialty cheese shops. If you can't find it, use pecorino or parmesan cheese with a good grinding of black pepper.

spaghetti with herbed ricotta

500g (1 pound) spaghetti

3 green onions (scallions)

2 cloves garlic

2¼ cups (540g) ricotta cheese

3 egg yolks

¾ cup (180ml) milk

⅓ cup coarsely chopped fresh flat-leaf parsley

¼ cup coarsely chopped fresh basil

¼ cup (20g) finely grated pepato cheese

1 Cook spaghetti in large saucepan of boiling water until tender; drain.
2 Meanwhile, chop onions finely. Crush garlic.
3 Whisk ricotta, egg yolks and milk in large bowl until smooth; stir in herbs, onion, garlic and pepato.
4 Add hot spaghetti to ricotta mixture; season to taste, toss gently.

prep + cook time 15 minutes
serves 4
nutritional count per serving
20.2g total fat
(10.8g saturated fat); 2809kJ
(672 cal); 89.4g carbohydrate;
30g protein; 4.9g fibre

mexican beef salad

35g (1-ounce) packet taco seasoning mix

600g (1¼-pound) piece beef rump steak

420g (13½ ounces) canned four-bean mix

125g (4 ounces) canned corn kernels

2 large tomatoes (440g)

½ cup coarsely chopped fresh coriander (cilantro)

1 medium lime (90g)

1 Rub seasoning mix over both sides of beef; cook beef in heated oiled large frying pan. Remove from pan; cover, stand 5 minutes then slice thickly.
2 Meanwhile, rinse and drain beans; drain corn. Chop tomatoes finely.
3 Combine beans, corn, tomato and coriander in medium bowl; season to taste.
4 Divide salad between serving plates; top with beef. Cut lime into wedges; serve with salad.

prep + cook time 15 minutes
serves 4
nutritional count per serving
10.7g total fat
(4.6g saturated fat); 1392kJ
(333 cal); 15.9g carbohydrate;
39.8g protein; 6.6g fibre

grilled chicken with thai pineapple

650g (1¼ pounds) chicken thigh fillets

½ small pineapple (450g)

½ cup loosely packed fresh mint leaves

1 fresh long red chilli

2 tablespoons lime juice

2 tablespoons fish sauce

1 Cook chicken on heated oiled grill plate (or grill or barbecue).
2 Meanwhile, peel and coarsely chop pineapple. Tear mint leaves. Slice chilli thinly.
3 Combine pineapple, mint and chilli in medium bowl with juice and sauce; season to taste.
4 Serve chicken with salad.

prep + cook time 15 minutes
serves 4
nutritional count per serving
11.4g total fat
(3.5g saturated fat); 1053kJ
(252 cal); 5.6g carbohydrate;
30.8g protein; 1.9g fibre

lemon tuna pasta

veal cutlets with pear and pistachio salsa

4 veal cutlets (500g)

1 medium orange (240g)

2 medium pears (460g)

¼ cup (35g) unsalted pistachios

⅓ cup finely chopped fresh flat-leaf parsley

1 tablespoon olive oil

1 Cook cutlets on heated oiled grill plate (or grill or barbecue).
2 Meanwhile, finely grate 1 teaspoon rind from orange. Squeeze ¼ cup juice from orange. Chop unpeeled pears finely. Chop nuts finely.
3 Combine rind, juice, pear, nuts, parsley and oil in medium bowl; season to taste.
4 Serve cutlets topped with salsa.

prep + cook time 15 minutes
serves 4
nutritional count per serving
11.4g total fat
(1.8g saturated fat); 1078kJ
(258 cal); 12.3g carbohydrate;
24.7g protein; 3.5g fibre

lemon tuna pasta

500g (1 pound) spaghetti

425g (13½ ounces) canned tuna in oil

⅔ cup (100g) drained semi-dried tomatoes in oil

1 medium lemon (140g)

50g (1½ ounces) baby rocket (arugula) leaves

½ cup (40g) shaved parmesan cheese

1 Cook spaghetti in large saucepan of boiling water until tender; drain.
2 Meanwhile, warm undrained tuna and tomatoes in medium saucepan.
3 Finely grate 1 teaspoon rind from lemon. Squeeze ¼ cup juice from lemon.
4 Combine hot spaghetti, tuna mixture, rind, juice and rocket in large bowl; season to taste. Serve sprinkled with cheese.

prep + cook time 15 minutes
serves 6
nutritional count per serving
20.9g total fat
(4.2g saturated fat); 2370kJ
(567 cal); 63g carbohydrate;
28.7g protein; 5.3g fibre

veal cutlets with pear and pistachio salsa

thai chicken burger

500g (1 pound) minced
(ground) chicken

1 egg

¼ cup finely chopped fresh
thai basil leaves

4 ciabatta rolls (460g)

2 tablespoons thai chilli jam

40g (1½ ounces) baby
asian greens

1 Combine chicken, egg and
basil in medium bowl, season;
shape into four patties.
2 Cook patties in heated
oiled large frying pan until
cooked through.
3 Meanwhile, split rolls in
half; toast cut sides until
lightly browned.
4 Sandwich rolls with chilli jam,
patties and greens.

prep + cook time 20 minutes
makes 4
nutritional count per burger
14.7g total fat
(3.9g saturated fat); 2094kJ
(501 cal); 53.7g carbohydrate;
35.6g protein; 4.1g fibre

tip Store-bought thai chilli jam
can be very hot, so use
according to taste or use sweet
chilli sauce, if you prefer.

spicy fish burgers

2 tablespoons peri peri spice mix

4 x 180g (5½-ounce) firm white fish fillets

1 baby cos (romaine) lettuce

½ cup (150g) mayonnaise

2 tablespoons finely chopped fresh dill

4 bread rolls (200g)

1 Sprinkle spice mix all over fish, season; cook fish in heated oiled large frying pan.

2 Meanwhile, separate lettuce leaves. Combine mayonnaise and dill in small bowl.

3 Split rolls in half; toast cut sides until lightly browned. Spread rolls with mayonnaise mixture. Sandwich rolls with lettuce leaves and fish.

prep + cook time 20 minutes
makes 4
nutritional count per burger
15.2g total fat
(2.5g saturated fat); 1726kJ
(413 cal); 26.5g carbohydrate;
40.9g protein; 2.7g fibre

steak with mushroom gravy

4 beef T-bone steaks (1.2kg)

250g (8 ounces) button mushrooms

1 tablespoon plain (all-purpose) flour

1¼ cups (310ml) beef stock

1 Season steaks; cook steaks in heated oiled large frying pan. Remove from pan; cover to keep warm.
2 Meanwhile, thinly slice mushrooms. Cook mushrooms in same heated pan, stirring, until tender. Add flour; cook, stirring, for 1 minute. Gradually stir in stock; cook, stirring until gravy boils and thickens.
3 Serve steaks with gravy.

prep + cook time 20 minutes
serves 4
nutritional count per serving
28.1g total fat (11.4g saturated fat); 1885kJ (451 cal); 3.4g carbohydrate; 45.7g protein; 1.7g fibre

tip Veal T-bone steaks can also be used.
serving suggestion Serve with roasted or mashed potatoes.

This dish could also be served as a starter. If you do, try not to follow it with a main course that's equally rich. Grilled plain chops or poached fish fillets would be nice.

gnocchi al quattro formaggi

¼ cup (60ml) dry white wine

1 cup (250g) mascarpone

⅓ cup (35g) coarsely grated mozzarella cheese

½ cup (40g) coarsely grated parmesan cheese

¼ cup (60ml) milk

625g (1¼ pounds) packaged potato gnocchi

75g (2½ ounces) gorgonzola cheese

¼ cup finely chopped fresh flat-leaf parsley

1 Place wine in large saucepan; boil, uncovered, until wine reduces by half. Reduce heat, add mascarpone; stir until mixture is smooth. Add mozzarella, parmesan and milk; cook, stirring, until cheeses melt and sauce is smooth.

2 Meanwhile, cook gnocchi in large saucepan of boiling water until gnocchi rise to the surface and are tender; drain.

3 Add gnocchi and crumbled gorgonzola to sauce; season to taste, toss gently to coat. Serve sprinkled with parsley.

prep + cook time 20 minutes
serves 4
nutritional count per serving
49g total fat
(31.8g saturated fat); 2993kJ
(716 cal); 47.3g carbohydrate;
17.8g protein; 3.6g fibre

ginger and teriyaki beef

2 tablespoons teriyaki sauce

2 tablespoons hoisin sauce

1 tablespoon mirin

1 large red capsicum
(bell pepper) (350g)

200g (6½ ounces) snow peas

1 medium carrot (120g)

115g (3½ ounces) baby corn

4cm (1½-inch) piece
fresh ginger (20g)

200g (6½ ounces) beef fillet

½ teaspoon peanut oil

2 tablespoons water

1 Combine sauces and mirin in small jug.
2 Thinly slice capsicum. Trim and thinly slice snow peas lengthways. Cut carrot into matchsticks. Quarter corn lengthways. Peel ginger; slice thinly. Thinly slice beef.
3 Heat oil in wok; stir-fry beef until browned. Remove from wok.
4 Add capsicum, peas, carrot, corn, ginger and the water to wok; stir-fry until carrot is almost tender. Return beef to wok with sauce mixture; stir-fry until hot. Season to taste.

prep + cook time 20 minutes
serves 4
nutritional count per serving
3.9g total fat
(1.1g saturated fat); 727kJ
(174 cal); 15.7g carbohydrate;
15.5g protein; 5.3g fibre

serving suggestion Serve with steamed jasmine rice.

lamb cutlets with tomato and coriander salsa

2 cloves garlic

2 medium (280g) lemons

1 teaspoon ground coriander

½ teaspoon ground cumin

1 teaspoon olive oil

12 french-trimmed lamb
cutlets (600g)

tomato and coriander salsa

2 small tomatoes (180g)

1 small red onion (100g)

1 clove garlic

1 tablespoon red wine vinegar

1 tablespoon finely chopped
fresh coriander (cilantro)

1 Crush garlic. Grate 2
tablespoons rind from lemons.
Squeeze ¼ cup juice from lemon.
Combine garlic, rind, juice, spices
and oil in small bowl; rub mixture
over cutlets, stand 10 minutes.
2 Meanwhile, make tomato and
coriander salsa.
3 Cook cutlets on heated oiled
barbecue (or grill or grill plate).
4 Serve cutlets topped with
tomato and coriander salsa.

**TOMATO AND CORIANDER
SALSA** Finely chop tomatoes
and onion. Crush garlic.
Combine all ingredients in small
bowl; season to taste.

prep + cook time 20 minutes
serves 4
nutritional count per serving
8.7g total fat
(3.6g saturated fat); 698kJ
(167 cal); 2.7g carbohydrate;
17.9g protein; 1.4g fibre

pork saltimbocca kebabs

satay pork medallions

4 pork loin steaks (600g)
....
¼ cup (70g) crunchy
peanut butter
....
⅓ cup (80ml) coconut cream
....
2 tablespoons sweet chilli sauce
....
2 teaspoons fish sauce
....
¼ cup (60ml) water
....
1 tablespoon coarsely chopped
fresh coriander (cilantro)
....

1 Cook pork on heated oiled
grill plate (or grill or barbecue).
2 Meanwhile, combine peanut
butter, coconut cream, sauces
and the water in small saucepan;
cook, stirring, about 3 minutes
or until thickened slightly. Season
to taste.
3 Serve pork drizzled with sauce;
sprinkle with coriander.

prep + cook time 15 minutes
serves 4
nutritional count per serving
23.9g total fat
(8.7g saturated fat); 1655kJ
(396 cal); 4.6g carbohydrate;
39.7g protein; 2.8g fibre

serving suggestion Serve
with steamed jasmine rice and
asian greens.

pork saltimbocca kebabs

650g (1¼ pounds) pork fillets
....
2 tablespoons coarsely
chopped fresh sage
....
8 slices prosciutto (120g)
....

1 Cut pork into 2.5cm (1-inch)
pieces. Combine pork and sage
in medium bowl; season.
2 Halve prosciutto lengthways.
Wrap half the pork pieces in
prosciutto; thread plain pork
pieces alternately with prosciutto-
wrapped pieces onto eight
skewers. Cook skewers on
heated oiled barbecue (or grill or
grill plate).

prep + cook time 20 minutes
makes 8
nutritional count per kebab
0.7g total fat
(0.2g saturated fat); 93kJ
(22 cal); 0g carbohydrate;
4.1g protein; 0g fibre

tip We used metal skewers but
you can use bamboo skewers;
cover the ends of the bamboo
skewers in foil to prevent
scorching during cooking. Or,
if you have the time, soak them
in cold water for 30 minutes
before use.

satay pork medallions

20
minute
sides

ruby grapefruit, pomegranate and endive salad

3 ruby red grapefruit (1kg)

¼ cup (60ml) olive oil

2 tablespoons coarsely chopped fresh chervil

100g (3 ounces) curly endive leaves

½ cup (125ml) pomegranate pulp

½ cup (55g) coarsely chopped roasted walnuts

1 Juice half of one grapefruit; reserve juice. Peel remaining grapefruit; slice thickly.
2 Place reserved juice, oil and chervil in screw-top jar, season to taste; shake well.
3 Place endive and dressing in large bowl; toss gently to combine.
4 Layer endive, grapefruit and pomegranate on serving plate; sprinkle with nuts.

prep time 15 minutes **serves** 4
nutritional count per serving
23.7g total fat
(2.5g saturated fat); 1208kJ
(289 cal); 12.8g carbohydrate;
4.5g protein; 4.6g fibre

tip You need one medium pomegranate for this recipe. Pomegranate pulp consists of the seeds and the edible pulp surrounding them; it has a tangy sweet-sour flavour. To remove the seeds, cut the fruit in half crossways and hold each half cut-side down over a bowl. Hit the outside skin of the fruit as hard as you can with a wooden spoon; the seeds should fall out but if they don't, dig them out with a teaspoon.

roasted truss tomatoes with basil

roasted truss tomatoes with basil

500g (1 pound) baby vine-ripened truss tomatoes

2 cloves garlic

1 tablespoon olive oil

2 teaspoons balsamic vinegar

vegetable oil, for deep-frying

⅓ cup loosely packed fresh basil leaves

1 Preheat oven to 180°C/350°F.
2 Place tomatoes on oven tray. Thinly slice garlic. Pour combined garlic, oil and vinegar over tomatoes, season. Roast, uncovered, about 10 minutes or until tomatoes soften.
3 Meanwhile, heat vegetable oil in small saucepan; deep-fry basil, in batches, until crisp. Drain on absorbent paper.
4 Serve tomatoes sprinkled with basil.

prep + cook time 20 minutes
serves 8
nutritional count per serving
4.6g total fat
(0.6g saturated fat); 213kJ
(51 cal); 1.5g carbohydrate;
0.4g protein; 1.2g fibre

steamed jasmine rice

steamed jasmine rice

1 cup (200g) jasmine rice

2 cups (500ml) water

1 Rinse rice under cold water until water runs clear; drain.
2 Bring the water to the boil, covered, in medium saucepan; add rice. Cook, covered, over low heat, 10 minutes. Remove from heat; stand, covered, 10 minutes. Fluff rice with fork; season to taste.

prep + cook time 20 minutes
serves 4
nutritional count per serving
0.3g total fat
(0g saturated fat); 752kJ
(180 cal); 39.9g carbohydrate;
3.3g protein; 1.1g fibre

pine nut & dried fig couscous

salad of herbs

½ small red onion (50g)

⅓ cup (55g) seeded mixed olives

60g (2 ounces) baby rocket (arugula) leaves

½ cup each loosely packed fresh flat-leaf parsley and coriander (cilantro) leaves

2 cups (230g) firmly packed trimmed watercress

preserved lemon dressing

1 clove garlic

1 tablespoon olive oil

¼ teaspoon sweet paprika

2 tablespoons lemon juice

1 tablespoon finely chopped preserved lemon rind

1 Make preserved lemon dressing.
2 Thinly slice onion; coarsely chop olives.
3 Place salad ingredients in large bowl with dressing, season to taste; toss gently to combine.

PRESERVED LEMON DRESSING
Crush garlic. Place ingredients in screw-top jar; season to taste, shake well.

prep time 15 minutes **serves** 4
nutritional count per serving
5.3g total fat
(0.7g saturated fat); 339kJ
(81 cal); 3.9g carbohydrate;
2.6g protein; 3.5g fibre

pine nut & dried fig couscous

1 cup (250ml) chicken stock

1 cup (200g) couscous

½ cup (80g) pine nuts

⅔ cup (130g) coarsely chopped dried figs

2 teaspoons finely grated lemon rind

¼ cup (60ml) lemon juice

¼ cup finely chopped fresh flat-leaf parsley

1 Bring stock to the boil in medium saucepan. Remove from heat, add couscous, cover; stand about 5 minutes or until liquid is absorbed, fluffing with fork occasionally.

2 Meanwhile, roast pine nuts in small frying pan until browned lightly. Stir remaining ingredients into couscous; season to taste.

prep + cook time 15 minutes
serves 4
nutritional count per serving
9.9g total fat
(0.7g saturated fat); 1179kJ
(282 cal); 38.5g carbohydrate;
7.4g protein; 4.2g fibre

tips Add your favourite dried fruit or nuts to the couscous. Serve warm or cold.

salad of herbs

creamy mashed potatoes

750g (1½ pounds) potatoes

60g (2 ounces) butter

½ cup (125ml) hot
pouring cream

1 Peel and coarsely chop
potatoes. Boil, steam or
microwave until tender; drain.
2 Mash potato with chopped
butter and cream in medium bowl
until smooth; season to taste.

prep + cook time 20 minutes
serves 6
nutritional count per serving
17.3g total fat
(11.4g saturated fat); 941kJ
(225 cal); 13.9g carbohydrate;
2.9g protein; 1.6g fibre

soft polenta

3 cups (750ml) water

2 cups (500ml) vegetable stock

2 cups (340g) polenta

1 cup (250ml) milk

30g (1 ounce) butter

¼ cup (20g) finely grated parmesan cheese

1 Bring the water and stock to the boil in large saucepan. Gradually stir in polenta. Reduce heat; simmer, stirring, about 10 minutes or until polenta thickens.
2 Add milk, butter and cheese; stir until cheese melts, season to taste.

prep + cook time 20 minutes
serves 6
nutritional count per serving
8.3g total fat
(4.8g saturated fat); 502kJ
(120 cal); 41.7g carbohydrate;
8.2g protein; 1.6g fibre

greek salad

1 clove garlic

¼ cup (60ml) olive oil

1 tablespoon lemon juice

1 tablespoon white
wine vinegar

1 tablespoon finely chopped
fresh oregano

3 medium tomatoes (450g)

2 lebanese cucumbers (260g)

200g (6½ ounces) fetta cheese

1 small red onion (100g)

1 small red capsicum
(bell pepper) (150g)

½ cup (75g) seeded black olives

1 Crush garlic. Whisk oil, juice, vinegar, oregano and garlic in large bowl.
2 Cut tomatoes into wedges; coarsely chop cucumbers and fetta. Thinly slice onion and capsicum.
3 Add all ingredients to bowl; toss gently to combine. Season to taste.

prep time 20 minutes serves 4
nutritional count per serving
25.8g total fat
(9.6g saturated fat); 1359kJ
(325 cal); 10.8g carbohydrate;
11.5g protein; 3.2g fibre

serving suggestion Serve with beef or lamb kebabs.

30 minute mains

cajun chicken burgers

2 chicken breast fillets (400g)

2 tablespoons cajun seasoning

⅓ cup (95g) yogurt

2 teaspoons finely grated lemon rind

1 medium tomato (150g)

1 shallot (25g)

½ small ripe avocado (100g)

4 crusty bread rolls (200g)

50g (1½ ounces) mesclun

1 Cut chicken in half horizontally; sprinkle all over with seasoning. Cook on heated oiled barbecue (or grill or grill plate).

2 Meanwhile, combine yogurt and rind in small bowl.

3 Finely chop tomato, shallot and avocado. Combine in separate small bowl; season to taste.

4 Cut rolls in half; toast, cut-sides down, on cleaned barbecue.

5 Sandwich mesclun, avocado mixture, chicken and yogurt mixture between rolls.

prep + cook time 30 minutes
makes 4
nutritional count per burger
12.9g total fat
(3.3g saturated fat); 1731kJ
(414 cal); 41.8g carbohydrate;
30.2g protein; 3.7g fibre

tip For fish burgers, replace the chicken with four 125g (4-ounce) firm white fish fillets.

honey prawns with pineapple

800g (1½ pounds) uncooked medium king prawns (shrimp)

1 large red capsicum (bell pepper) (350g)

½ small pineapple (450g)

155g (5 ounces) snow peas

2 cloves garlic

230g (7 ounces) canned bamboo shoots

1 teaspoon peanut oil

2 tablespoons tamarind concentrate

2 tablespoons kecap manis

1 tablespoon honey

1 Shell and devein prawns, leaving tails intact.
2 Coarsely chop capsicum and pineapple. Trim snow peas; crush garlic. Rinse and drain bamboo shoots.
3 Heat oil in wok; stir-fry prawns, capsicum, peas and garlic until prawns have changed colour.
4 Add remaining ingredients; stir-fry until hot. Season to taste.

prep + cook time 30 minutes
serves 4
nutritional count per serving
2g total fat
(0.3g saturated fat); 807kJ
(193 cal); 16.7g carbohydrate;
24.3g protein; 4g fibre
serving suggestion Serve with steamed jasmine rice.

sesame crusted tuna
with grape and lychee salad

½ cup (75g) white sesame seeds

½ cup (75g) black sesame seeds

½ cup (100g) white
long-grain rice

1kg (2-pound) piece tuna loin

¼ cup (60ml) honey
mustard sauce

grape and lychee salad

565g (1¼ pounds)
canned lychees

250g (8 ounces) seedless
black grapes

2 fresh long red chillies

40g (1½ ounces) trimmed
watercress sprigs

¾ cup loosely packed fresh
mint leaves

2 tablespoons lime juice

2 tablespoons olive oil

1 Make grape and lychee salad.
2 Dry-fry seeds, separately, in medium frying pan until toasted; remove from pan. Add rice to pan, dry-fry until toasted lightly.
3 Blend or process rice and white sesame seeds 2 minutes or until powdery. Combine powder in small bowl with black sesame seeds.
4 Trim tuna. Cook tuna on heated oiled barbecue (or grill or grill plate) about 8 minutes or until browned all over. Remove from barbecue; cover, stand 10 minutes.
5 Coat tuna with honey mustard sauce. Place tuna on tray; coat with sesame mixture.
6 Slice tuna; serve with salad.

GRAPE AND LYCHEE SALAD
Drain lychees; halve lychees and grapes. Thinly slice chillies. Place all ingredients in large bowl; toss gently to combine. Season to taste.

prep + cook time 30 minutes
serves 6
nutritional count per serving
30.1g total fat
(6.5g saturated fat); 2504kJ
(599 cal); 29.8g carbohydrate;
50.6g protein; 4.6g fibre

lemon fish parcels

moroccan fish with almond couscous

1 cup (200g) couscous
1 cup (250ml) boiling water
1 cup (80g) flaked almonds
2 tablespoons moroccan spice mix
4 x 180g (5½-ounce) white fish fillets
2 tablespoons finely chopped fresh mint
⅔ cup (190g) yogurt

lemon fish parcels

425g (13½ ounces) canned peeled baby potatoes
340g (11 ounces) asparagus
4 x 200g (6½-ounce) white fish fillets
¼ cup (60ml) lemon juice
1 tablespoon olive oil

1 Preheat oven to 200°C/400°F.
2 Rinse and drain potatoes; halve. Trim asparagus.
3 Place four large squares of baking paper on top of four large squares of foil. Layer potato and asparagus on squares; top with fish. Drizzle with juice and oil; season.

4 Fold parcels to enclose fish in foil; place on oven tray.
5 Bake parcels about 15 minutes.

prep + cook time 30 minutes
serves 4
nutritional count per serving
9.1g total fat (2g saturated fat); 1271kJ (304 cal); 10g carbohydrate; 43.9g protein; 2.1g fibre

serving suggestion Serve with baby spinach leaves and lemon wedges.

1 Combine couscous with the boiling water in medium heatproof bowl. Cover; stand 5 minutes or until liquid is absorbed, fluffing with fork occasionally.
2 Meanwhile, roast nuts in small frying pan until browned lightly. Stir nuts into couscous; season to taste.
3 Rub spice mix all over fish. Cook fish in heated oiled large frying pan. Break fish into chunks.
4 Combine mint and yogurt in small bowl.
5 Serve fish with couscous and minted yogurt.

prep + cook time 25 minutes
serves 4
nutritional count per serving
17.2g total fat (3.1g saturated fat); 2224kJ (532 cal); 42.6g carbohydrate; 49.7g protein; 2.7g fibre

moroccan fish with almond couscous

mexican chicken pizza

600g (1¼ pounds) chicken tenderloins

35g (1 ounce) taco seasoning mix

8 x 60g (2-ounce) small pizza bases

300g (9½ ounces) bottled chunky tomato salsa

2 cups (220g) pizza cheese

1 medium avocado (250g)

1 Preheat oven to 220°C/425°F.
2 Combine chicken and seasoning mix in medium bowl. Cook chicken in heated oiled large frying pan.
3 Place pizza bases on oven trays; spread with salsa. Top with chicken; sprinkle with cheese.
4 Bake pizzas about 15 minutes or until cheese is browned lightly.
5 Meanwhile, thinly slice avocado. Serve pizza topped with avocado and, if you like, some baby rocket (arugula) leaves.

prep + cook time 30 minutes
makes 8
nutritional count per pizza
17.1g total fat
(6.6g saturated fat); 1797kJ
(430 cal); 36g carbohydrate;
31.1g protein; 3.5g fibre

grilled lemon chicken with crushed potatoes

1kg (2 pounds) baby
new potatoes

½ cup (125ml) pouring cream

½ cup coarsely chopped fresh
flat-leaf parsley

1 clove garlic

1 medium lemon (140g)

12 chicken tenderloins (900g)

1 Boil, steam or microwave potatoes until tender; drain.
2 Mash half the potatoes with cream until almost smooth. Coarsely crush remaining potatoes with the back of a fork until skins burst; fold into mashed potatoes with parsley. Season to taste.
3 Meanwhile, crush garlic. Finely grate 1 teaspoon rind from lemon. Cut lemon into wedges. Combine garlic, rind and chicken in medium bowl; season. Cook chicken on heated oiled grill plate (or grill or barbecue).
4 Serve chicken with potatoes and lemon wedges. Drizzle with a little extra olive oil, if you like.

prep + cook time 30 minutes
serves 4
nutritional count per serving
26.2g total fat
(12.2g saturated fat); 2516kJ
(602 cal); 33.8g carbohydrate;
54.9g protein; 5.5g fibre

barbecued salmon with minted peas and beans

2 medium limes (180g)

4 x 155g (5-ounce) salmon fillets

155g (5 ounces) green beans

1 cup (120g) frozen peas

⅓ cup finely chopped fresh mint

½ cup (125ml) buttermilk

1 Finely grate 2 teaspoons rind from limes; squeeze 1 tablespoon juice from limes.

2 Rub salmon all over with rind; cook salmon on heated oiled barbecue (or grill or grill plate).

3 Meanwhile, trim beans; chop coarsely. Boil, steam or microwave beans and peas, separately, until tender; drain. Combine beans, peas and half the mint in medium bowl; season to taste.

4 Combine buttermilk, lime juice and remaining mint in small jug; season to taste.

5 Serve bean mixture with fish; drizzle with buttermilk dressing.

prep + cook time 25 minutes
serves 4
nutritional count per serving
11.9g total fat
(2.9g saturated fat); 1129kJ
(270 cal); 4.7g carbohydrate;
34.4g protein; 3.1g fibre

chilli jam beef noodles

250g (8 ounces) dried rice stick noodles

625g (1¼ pounds) beef eye fillet

1 medium red capsicum (bell pepper) (200g)

155g (5 ounces) sugar snap peas

2 tablespoons thai chilli jam

¼ cup (60ml) water

½ cup loosely packed thai basil leaves

1 Place noodles in large heatproof bowl, cover with boiling water; stand until tender, drain.
2 Meanwhile, thinly slice beef and capsicum. Trim peas.
3 Combine beef and half the chilli jam in medium bowl.
4 Stir-fry beef mixture, in batches, in heated oiled wok until browned. Remove from wok.
5 Add capsicum to wok; stir-fry until tender. Return beef to wok with noodles, peas, the water and remaining chilli jam; stir-fry until hot. Season to taste; serve sprinkled with basil.

prep + cook time 25 minutes
serves 4
nutritional count per serving
9.9g total fat
(4g saturated fat); 1195kJ
(286 cal); 12.2g carbohydrate;
35.6g protein; 2.1g fibre

tips Thai basil, also called horapa, has a slight licorice or aniseed taste. Use sweet basil if thai basil is unavailable. Store-bought thai chilli jam can be very hot, so use according to taste or use sweet chilli sauce, if you prefer.

harissa lamb with orange couscous

410g (13 ounces)
lamb backstraps

1 tablespoon harissa paste

1 teaspoon ground cumin

2 medium oranges (480g)

1½ cups (300g) couscous

1½ cups (375ml) boiling water

½ cup coarsely chopped
fresh mint

1 Combine lamb, harissa and cumin in medium bowl. Cook lamb on heated oiled grill plate (or grill or barbecue). Remove from pan; cover, stand 5 minutes then slice thinly.

2 Meanwhile, finely grate 2 teaspoons rind from oranges; segment oranges over small bowl, reserving 2 tablespoons juice.

3 Combine couscous, rind and the water in large heatproof bowl. Cover; stand about 5 minutes or until water is absorbed, fluffing with fork occasionally. Stir in orange segments, reserved juice and mint; season to taste.

4 Serve lamb with couscous.

prep + cook time 25 minutes
serves 4
nutritional count per serving
9.8g total fat
(4.2g saturated fat); 2048kJ
(490 cal); 65.8g carbohydrate;
32.2g protein; 3.1g fibre

We used red sensation pears to add colour to this dish. They have a distinctive red and gold tone and a sweet, buttery flesh. Pork loin chops are also suitable for this recipe. If you have time, you can marinate the cutlets, covered, in the refrigerator, for 2 hours or overnight.

barbecued honey mustard pork cutlets

4 pork cutlets (940g)

2 tablespoons peanut oil

2 tablespoons honey

2 tablespoons dijonnaise

1 large pear (330g)

60g (2 ounces) mixed salad leaves

1 Combine pork, oil, honey and dijonnaise in large bowl; season.
2 Cook pork on heated oiled barbecue (or grill or grill plate).
3 Cut unpeeled pear into long thin strips. Place pear and salad leaves in medium bowl; toss gently to combine.
4 Serve pork with salad.

prep + cook time 25 minutes
serves 4
nutritional count per serving
26.2g total fat
(7.1g saturated fat); 1777kJ
(425 cal); 19.9g carbohydrate;
26.8g protein; 2.2g fibre
serving suggestion Serve with lemon wedges.

ginger chilli pork with pears

4 x 300g (9½-ounce) pork loin chops

2 small pears (360g)

1 medium red onion (170g)

2cm (¾-inch) piece fresh ginger (10g)

½ cup (125ml) sweet chilli sauce

2 tablespoons lemon juice

1 Season pork. Cook pork in heated oiled large frying pan; remove from pan, cover to keep warm.
2 Meanwhile, halve unpeeled pears. Cut onion into thin wedges. Grate ginger.
3 Cook pear halves then onion in same pan until browned. Add ginger, sauce and juice to pan; simmer 2 minutes.
4 Serve pork with pear and onion mixture; drizzle with sauce.

prep + cook time 25 minutes
serves 4
nutritional count per serving
22g total fat
(7.3g saturated fat); 1806kJ
(432 cal); 19.8g carbohydrate;
36.9g protein; 4.1g fibre

serving suggestion Serve with mixed salad leaves.

italian-style lamb cutlets

8 french-trimmed lamb
cutlets (400g)

100g (3 ounces) goat's cheese

¼ cup (35g) finely chopped
sun-dried tomatoes

2 tablespoons finely shredded
fresh basil

8 slices prosciutto (120g)

1 Cut a small horizontal slit
in the side of each cutlet.
Combine crumbled cheese,
tomato and basil in medium
bowl; press cheese mixture into
lamb pockets.
2 Wrap each cutlet with a slice
of prosciutto. Cook cutlets in
heated oiled large frying pan until
cooked through.

prep + cook time 30 minutes
serves 4
nutritional count per serving
11g total fat
(5.4g saturated fat); 828kJ
(198 cal); 3.4g carbohydrate;
20.8g protein; 1.3g fibre

serving suggestion Serve with a
green salad.

cheesy polenta with ratatouille

1 medium eggplant (300g)

1 large red capsicum
(bell pepper) (350g)

400g (12½ ounces) canned
diced tomatoes

¼ cup loosely packed fresh
baby basil leaves

cheesy polenta

1.25 litres (5 cups) water

1 cup (170g) polenta

1 cup (80g) finely grated
parmesan cheese

1 Coarsely chop eggplant
and capsicum. Cook eggplant
and capsicum in heated oiled
large frying pan until tender.
Add undrained tomatoes;
simmer, uncovered, 5 minutes
or until mixture thickens slightly.
Season to taste.

2 Meanwhile, make
cheesy polenta.

3 Serve polenta with ratatouille;
sprinkle with basil.

CHEESY POLENTA Bring
the water to the boil in large
saucepan; gradually stir in
polenta. Reduce heat; cook,
stirring, about 10 minutes or
until polenta thickens.
Remove from heat; stir in
cheese. Season to taste. Stand
3 minutes before serving.

prep + cook time 30 minutes
serves 4
nutritional count per serving
7.9g total fat
(4.2g saturated fat); 1208kJ
(289 cal); 37.5g carbohydrate;
14g protein; 5.3g fibre

spicy squid and tomato linguine

375g (12 ounces) linguine pasta

2 cloves garlic

1 teaspoon dried chilli flakes

800g (1½ pounds) canned crushed tomatoes

500g (1 pound) cleaned squid hoods

30g (1 ounce) baby rocket (arugula) leaves

1 Cook pasta in large saucepan of boiling water until tender; drain.

2 Meanwhile, crush garlic. Cook garlic and chilli flakes in heated oiled large frying pan, stirring, until fragrant. Add undrained tomatoes; bring to the boil. Reduce heat; simmer, uncovered, about 10 minutes or until sauce thickens slightly.

3 Slice squid thinly. Add squid to tomato sauce; cook, stirring occasionally, about 5 minutes or until squid is tender. Season to taste.

4 Combine hot pasta with sauce; serve topped with rocket.

prep + cook time 25 minutes
serves 4
nutritional count per serving
3g total fat
(0.7g saturated fat); 1919kJ
(459 cal); 70.5g carbohydrate;
33.3g protein; 5.9g fibre

This sauce is named after the Roman restaurateur Alfredo di Lello who created the dish in the 1920s. Do not reduce the cream too rapidly, or by too much, as it can burn. Check and stir once or twice and take the pan off the heat when it has reduced correctly.

fettuccine alfredo

500g (1 pound) fresh
fettuccine pasta

80g (2½ ounces) butter

1¼ cups (300ml) pouring cream

½ cup (40g) finely grated
parmesan cheese

2 tablespoons coarsely chopped
fresh flat-leaf parsley

1 Cook pasta in large saucepan of boiling water until tender; drain. Return to pan.

2 Meanwhile, melt chopped butter in medium frying pan, add cream; bring to the boil. Reduce heat; simmer, uncovered, about 5 minutes or until sauce reduces by half. Add cheese; stir over low heat about 2 minutes or until cheese melts.

3 Add sauce to pasta; toss gently to coat, season to taste. Sprinkle with parsley.

prep + cook time 25 minutes
serves 4
nutritional count per serving
53.4g total fat
(34.5g saturated fat); 3821kJ
(914 cal); 87.5g carbohydrate;
19.4g protein; 4.1g fibre

spaghetti with pesto

2 tablespoons pine nuts

2 cups coarsely chopped fresh basil

2 cloves garlic

⅓ cup (80ml) olive oil

¼ cup (20g) finely grated parmesan cheese

375g (12 ounces) spaghetti

1 Roast nuts in small frying pan until browned lightly. Blend or process nuts, basil and peeled garlic until smooth. With motor operating, add oil in a thin steady stream; process until mixture is combined. Place pesto in medium bowl; stir in cheese, season to taste.
2 Cook spaghetti in large saucepan of boiling water until tender; drain.
3 Combine spaghetti and pesto in large bowl.

prep + cook time 25 minutes
serves 4
nutritional count per serving
26g total fat
(4.1g saturated fat); 2328kJ
(557 cal); 65g carbohydrate;
13.7g protein; 4.3g fibre

serving suggestion Top with flaked parmesan.

30 minute sides

vietnamese coleslaw

2 medium carrots (240g)

½ small green papaya (325g)

1 cup (150g) crushed peanuts

6 cups (480g) coarsely shredded wombok (napa cabbage)

1 cup each firmly packed fresh mint and coriander (cilantro) leaves

lime dressing

1 clove garlic

1 fresh long red chilli

¼ cup (60ml) lime juice

2 tablespoons grated palm sugar

2 tablespoons fish sauce

2 teaspoons peanut oil

1 Cut carrot and papaya into matchsticks.
2 Roast nuts in small frying pan until browned lightly.
3 Make lime dressing.
4 Place all ingredients in large bowl with dressing; toss gently to combine, season to taste.

LIME DRESSING Crush garlic; chop chilli finely. Place all ingredients in screw-top jar; shake well.

prep + cook time 25 minutes
serves 8
nutritional count per serving
9.8g total fat
(1.4g saturated fat); 660kJ
(158 cal); 9.4g carbohydrate;
6.2g protein; 4.6g fibre

tips Coleslaw is best dressed just before serving. You need a wombok weighing about 1.2kg (2½ pounds) for this recipe.

roasted beetroot and orange salad

1kg (2 pounds) baby
beetroots (beets)

2 medium oranges (480g)

75g (2½ ounces) baby
spinach leaves

½ cup (55g) coarsely chopped
roasted walnuts

1 tablespoon white
wine vinegar

2 teaspoons caraway seeds

1 Preheat oven to 240°C/475°F.
2 Trim beetroot. Wrap beetroot
in foil; place in small shallow
baking dish. Roast about
20 minutes or until tender.
When cool enough to handle,
peel and halve beetroot.
3 Meanwhile, segment oranges
over small bowl; reserve ¼ cup
of the juice.
4 Place beetroot, orange
segments and reserved juice in
large bowl with remaining
ingredients; toss gently to
combine, season to taste.

prep + cook time 30 minutes
serves 4
nutritional count per serving
9.9g total fat
(0.6g saturated fat); 1032kJ
(247 cal); 27.1g carbohydrate;
7.6g protein; 9.9g fibre

Wear gloves when peeling beetroot to stop the juice from
staining your hands.

You will need one bunch of red radishes for this recipe. This recipe is best made just before serving; it will become soggy if left standing.

orange and radish salad

4 medium oranges (960g)

500g (1 pound) red radishes

1 tablespoon olive oil

2 teaspoons white wine vinegar

¼ cup finely chopped fresh mint

1 Finely grate 2 teaspoons rind from an orange. Segment oranges over small bowl; reserve 1 tablespoon juice.

2 Trim radishes. Using mandoline or V-slicer, slice radishes as thinly as possible.

3 Whisk reserved juice, oil and vinegar in medium bowl. Add rind, orange segments, radish and mint; toss gently to combine, season to taste. Serve immediately.

prep + cook time 25 minutes
serves 4
nutritional count per serving
5g total fat
(0.6g saturated fat); 535kJ
(128 cal); 15.6g carbohydrate;
2.7g protein; 4.8g fibre

sesame patty-pan squash and sugar snap peas

300g (9½ ounces) sugar snap peas

16 yellow patty-pan squash (480g)

1 tablespoon sesame seeds

2 teaspoons sesame oil

1 tablespoon light soy sauce

1 Trim peas. Boil, steam or microwave peas and squash, separately, until tender; drain.

2 Meanwhile, toast seeds in small frying pan until browned lightly.

3 Place vegetables and seeds in large bowl with remaining ingredients; toss gently to combine, season to taste.

prep + cook time 25 minutes
serves 8
nutritional count per serving
2.1g total fat
(0.3g saturated fat); 213kJ
(51 cal); 3.8g carbohydrate;
3.1g protein; 2.4g fibre

gingered beans with peas and spinach

350g (11 ounces) green beans

100g (3 ounces) baby spinach leaves

2 cloves garlic

3cm (1¼-inch) piece fresh ginger (15g)

¼ cup (60ml) olive oil

½ teaspoon red chilli flakes

1 cup (120g) frozen baby green peas

1 Trim beans. Boil, steam or microwave beans until tender; drain. Rinse beans under cold water, drain; pat dry with absorbent paper.
2 Meanwhile, wash spinach; drain. Peel and slice garlic thinly. Cut peeled ginger into fine matchsticks.
3 Heat oil in wok; stir-fry garlic, ginger and chilli about 30 seconds or until fragrant. Add beans, spinach and peas; stir-fry about 1 minute or until spinach wilts and peas heat through. Season.

prep + cook time 25 minutes
serves 6
nutritional count per serving
9.4g total fat
(1.3g saturated fat); 477kJ
(114 cal); 2.9g carbohydrate;
2.9g protein; 3.8g fibre

grilled sweet potato salad

1 small kumara
(orange sweet potato) (250g)

1 small purple
sweet potato (250g)

1 small white
sweet potato (250g)

¼ cup (35g) roasted
macadamias

2 tablespoons coarsely
chopped fresh flat-leaf parsley

sherry vinegar dressing

2 tablespoons sherry vinegar

2 tablespoons macadamia oil

1 Thickly slice unpeeled kumara, purple sweet potato and white sweet potato.
2 Boil, steam or microwave sweet potatoes until almost tender; drain.
3 Meanwhile, chop nuts coarsely.
4 Make sherry vinegar dressing.
5 Cook potato slices on heated oiled grill plate (or grill or barbecue) until browned and tender.
6 Place potatoes on serving platter. Drizzle with dressing; sprinkle with parsley and nuts.

SHERRY VINEGAR DRESSING
Place ingredients in screw-top jar; shake well, season to taste.

prep + cook time 30 minutes
serves 4
nutritional count per serving
16.1g total fat
(2.2g saturated fat); 1187kJ
(284 cal);28.8g carbohydrate;
4g protein; 4.1g fibre

tip You could use olive oil instead of macadamia oil.

pilaf

warm kipfler potato salad

1kg (2 pounds) kipfler potatoes

1 small red onion (100g)

¼ cup (60ml) olive oil

1 teaspoon finely grated lemon rind

1 tablespoon lemon juice

2 teaspoons wholegrain mustard

1 cup loosely packed fresh flat-leaf parsley

1 Halve potatoes lengthways. Boil, steam or microwave potato until tender; drain.
2 Meanwhile, thinly slice onion.
3 Whisk oil, rind, juice and mustard in large bowl; mix in potatoes, onion and parsley. Season to taste.

prep + cook time 30 minutes
serves 4
nutritional count per serving
14g total fat
(1.9g saturated fat); 1267kJ
(303 cal); 34.4g carbohydrate;
6.8g protein; 6.2g fibre

pilaf

1 clove garlic

30g (1 ounce) butter

1 cup (200g) basmati rice

1 cup (250ml) chicken stock

1 cup (250ml) water

¼ cup (20g) flaked almonds

¼ cup coarsely chopped fresh flat-leaf parsley

1 Crush garlic. Heat butter in medium saucepan; cook garlic, stirring, until fragrant. Add rice; cook, stirring, 1 minute. Add stock and the water; bring to the boil. Reduce heat; simmer, covered, about 20 minutes or until rice is tender.

2 Meanwhile, roast nuts in small frying pan until browned lightly.
3 Remove from heat; fluff rice with fork. Stir in parsley and nuts; season to taste.

prep + cook time 30 minutes
serves 4
nutritional count per serving
9.4g total fat
(4.4g saturated fat); 1129kJ
(270 cal); 40.4g carbohydrate;
5.2g protein; 1.1g fibre

warm kipfler potato salad

cooking techniques

Washing leeks removes any grit from the inside layers. Cut in half lengthwise, stopping at the root. Fan the layers out and wash under fast-running cold water.

To prepare asparagus, snap the woody end off the asparagus by holding it close to the base and bending it until it snaps. Discard the woody end. Trim asparagus with a vegetable peeler.

To trim beetroot, cut the stems to 2cm (¾-inch) off the bulb, and don't trim the root at the base of the plant. This stops the colour from bleeding during cooking.

To grate beetroot, use the course (large) holes of the grater. It's best to wear disposable gloves as the juice can stain your hands.

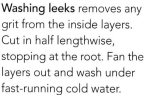

When cutting a chilli on the diagonal, leave it whole. The seeds are the heat source, so if you are intolerant of high heat levels, remove the seeds and membranes, or use less chilli.

To grate ginger, peel the piece of ginger with a vegetable peeler or small knife, cutting away awkward knobs and creases. Use the small holes on a box grater, or a rasp grater (thin metal graters), such as a Microplane grater (pictured above), to finely grate the ginger.

To crush garlic, press unpeeled garlic firmly with the side of a large knife (top) crushing the clove. Pull off the papery skin and chop the clove finely with the knife. A garlic press (bottom) removes and leaves the skin behind while crushing the garlic.

To use fresh thyme leaves, hold the top of the stem with one hand and run the fingers of the other hand down the stem to strip off the leaves. Any small, thin stems that break away with the leaves are fine to use.

To chop shallots, cut in half through the root. Make horizontal and vertical cuts in each half, but don't cut all the way through; chop finely.

To crush, grind or blend spices in a mortar and pestle, first place them in the mortar (bowl) then pound them vigorously with the pestle until they are as coarse or as fine as needed.

To slice a capsicum, cut the top and bottom off and stand it on one end; slice down removing all the flesh. Remove and discard the seeds and membranes, and slice the flesh.

Chiffonade is a way of cutting green leaves into long, thin strips. Lay leaves flat on top of each other, then roll up tightly and cut into thin slices.

Pitting an olive is easy with an olive pitter, pictured; just put the olive in the cup and push, and out pops the seed. To do this by hand, crush the olive with the flat side of a large knife and slip the seed out. The olives will then be easy to chop.

To peel a prawn, hold the body with one hand, twist the head with the other and pull it away from the body. Roll the shell, with the legs still attached, from the underside off the body. If removing the tail, squeeze the tail on both sides to release the shell from the flesh and remove.

To cut an onion into wedges, cut the onion in half lengthways through the root. Remove the papery outer skin. Lie the onion cut-side down and cut the onion lengthways through the root into triangular-shaped wedges. The root holds the wedges together.

To cut a cauliflower into florets, remove the leaves, then cut and remove most of the core. Cut off the florets where they join the centre core. Cut into any size you like by simply cutting through the stem and head of each floret. You can also break the florets off the core using your hands.

glossary

ALMONDS
flaked paper-thin slices.
ground also called almond meal.
slivered small pieces cut lengthways.

BASIL an aromatic herb; there are many types, but the most commonly used is sweet, or common, basil.
thai also called horapa; different from sweet basil in both look and taste, has smaller leaves and purplish stems. Has a light licorice or aniseed taste, and is one of the basic flavours that typify Thai cuisine.

BAY LEAVES aromatic leaves from the bay tree available fresh or dried; adds a strong, slightly peppery flavour.

BEAN SPROUTS tender new growths of assorted beans and seeds grown for consumption as sprouts.

BEANS
borlotti also called roman beans or pink beans, can be eaten fresh or dried. Interchangeable with pinto beans as they look similar – pale pink or beige with dark red streaks.

BEEF
eye-fillet tenderloin, fillet; fine texture, most expensive and very tender.
minced also called ground beef.
new-york cut boneless striploin steak.
rump boneless tender cut taken from the upper part of the round (hindquarter). Cut into steaks, good for barbecuing; as one piece, great as a roast.
T-bone sirloin steak with bone in and fillet eye attached.

BEETROOT (BEETS) also called red beets; firm, round root vegetable.

BUTTER we use salted butter unless stated otherwise; 125g is equal to 1 stick (4 ounces).

CAPERS the grey-green buds of a warm climate (usually Mediterranean) shrub, sold either dried and salted or pickled in a vinegar brine. Their pungent taste adds piquancy to a tapenade, sauces and condiments.

CAPSICUM (BELL PEPPER) also called pepper. Discard seeds and membranes before use.

CARAWAY SEEDS the small, half-moon-shaped dried seed from a member of the parsley family; adds a sharp anise flavour when used in both sweet and savoury dishes.

CARDAMOM a spice native to India and used extensively in its cuisine; can be purchased in pod, seed or ground form. Has a distinctive aromatic, sweetly rich flavour and is one of the world's most expensive spices.

CHEESE
fetta Greek in origin; a crumbly textured goat's- or sheep's-milk cheese with a sharp, salty taste. Ripened and stored in salted whey; particularly good cubed and tossed into salads.
goat's made from goat's milk, has an earthy, strong taste. Available in soft, crumbly and firm textures, in various shapes and sizes, and sometimes rolled in ash or herbs.
gorgonzola a creamy Italian blue cheese with a mild, sweet taste; good as an accompaniment to fruit or used to flavour sauces (especially pasta).
mozzarella soft, spun-curd cheese; originating in southern Italy where it was traditionally made from water-buffalo milk. Now generally made from cow's milk.
parmesan also called parmigiano; is a hard, grainy cow's-milk cheese originating in the Parma region of Italy.
pepato an Italian sheep's milk cheese, most often pecorino, studded with peppercorns. It is available from some delicatessens and specialty cheese shops. If you can't find it, use pecorino or parmesan cheese with a good grinding of black pepper.
pizza cheese a commercial blend of varying proportions of processed grated mozzarella, cheddar and parmesan cheeses.
ricotta a soft, sweet, moist, white cow's-milk cheese with a low fat content (8.5 per cent) and a slightly grainy texture.

CHERVIL also called cicily; mildly fennel-flavoured member of the parsley family with curly dark-green leaves.

CHICKEN
breast fillet breast halved, skinned and boned.
tenderloin thin strip of meat lying just under the breast; good for stir-frying.
thigh skin and bone intact.
thigh fillet thigh with skin and centre bone removed.

CHILLI use rubber gloves when seeding and chopping fresh chillies as they can burn your skin. Removing the seeds lessens the heat level.

CINNAMON available in sticks (also called quills) and ground.

CORIANDER (CILANTRO) also called pak chee or chinese parsley; bright-green-leafed herb with a pungent aroma and taste.

CORNFLOUR (CORNSTARCH) available made from corn or wheat; used as a thickening agent in cooking.

CREAM
pouring also called pure or fresh cream. It has no additives and contains a minimum fat content of 35 per cent.
sour cream a thick, commercially-cultured sour cream with a minimum fat content of 35 per cent.
thickened a whipping cream that contains a thickener. It has a minimum fat content of 35 per cent.

CUMIN also called zeera or comino; resembling caraway in size, cumin is the dried seed of a plant related to the parsley family. Its spicy, almost curry-like flavour is essential to the traditional foods of Mexico, India, North Africa and the Middle East. Available dried as seeds or ground.

CURRY PASTE various ready-made pastes are available from the supermarket. The heat intensity of may differ from brand to brand, so adjust the amount used according to your taste.

DILL also called dill weed; used fresh or dried, in seed form or ground. Has an anise/celery sweetness. Its feathery, frond-like fresh leaves are grassier and more subtle than the dried version or the seeds.

DUKKAH an Egyptian specialty spice mixture made up of roasted nuts, seeds and an array of aromatic spices.

EGGPLANT also called aubergine.

FENUGREEK hard, dried seed usually sold ground as an astringent spice powder. Good with seafood and in chutneys.

GAI LAN also called gai larn, chinese broccoli and chinese kale; green vegetable appreciated more for its stems than its coarse leaves. Can be served steamed and stir-fried, in soups and noodle dishes. One of the most popular Asian greens.

HARISSA a North African paste made from dried red chillies, garlic, olive oil and caraway seeds; can be used as a rub for meat, an ingredient in sauces and dressings, or eaten as a condiment. It is available from Middle Eastern food shops and some supermarkets.

HOISIN SAUCE a thick, sweet and spicy Chinese barbecue sauce made from salted fermented soybeans, onions and garlic; used as a marinade or baste, or to accent stir-fries and barbecued or roasted foods. From Asian food shops and supermarkets.

KECAP MANIS a dark, thick sweet soy sauce used in most South-East Asian cuisines. Depending on the manufacturer, the sauces' sweetness is derived from the addition of either molasses or palm sugar when brewed.

KUMARA the Polynesian name of an orange-fleshed sweet potato often confused with yam; good baked, boiled, mashed or fried similarly to other potatoes.

LAMB
backstrap also called eye of loin; the larger fillet from a row of loin chops or cutlets. Tender, best cooked rapidly: barbecued or pan-fried.
cutlet small, tender rib chop; sometimes sold french-trimmed, with all the fat and gristle at the narrow end of the bone removed.

LENTILS (red, brown, yellow) dried pulses often identified by and named after their colour. Eaten by cultures all over the world, most famously perhaps in the dhals of India, lentils have high food value.

MESCLUN pronounced mess-kluhn; also known as mixed greens or spring salad mix. A commercial blend of assorted young lettuce and other green leaves, including baby spinach leaves, mizuna and curly endive.

MIRIN a Japanese champagne-coloured cooking wine, made of glutinous rice and alcohol. It is used expressly for cooking and should not be confused with sake.

MOROCCAN SEASONING contains turmeric, cumin and cinnamon and adds an authentic Moroccan flavouring; available from most Middle Eastern food stores, spice shops and major supermarkets.

MUSHROOMS
button small, cultivated white mushrooms with a mild flavour. When we call for an unspecified type of mushroom, use button.

NOODLES, DRIED RICE also called rice stick noodles. Made from rice flour and water, available flat and wide or very thin (vermicelli). Must be soaked in boiling water to soften.

NUTMEG a strong and pungent spice ground from the dried nut of an evergreen tree native to Indonesia. Usually found ground but the flavour is more intense from a whole nut, available from spice shops, so it's best to grate your own. Used most often in baking and milk-based desserts, but also works nicely in savoury dishes. Found in mixed spice mixtures.

OYSTER SAUCE Asian in origin, this thick, richly flavoured brown sauce is made from oysters and their brine, cooked with salt and soy sauce, and thickened with starches. Use as a condiment.

PAPAYA the papaya family includes the yellow-fleshed fruit called pawpaw and the pink-fleshed fruit, papaya.

PAPRIKA ground dried sweet red capsicum (bell pepper); there are many grades and types available, including sweet, hot, mild and smoked.

PEPITAS are the pale green kernels of dried pumpkin seeds; they can be bought plain or salted.

PERI PERI SAUCE (also called piri-piri) a Portuguese chilli sauce made from red chillies, ginger, garlic, oil and various herbs.

PLUM SAUCE a thick, sweet and sour dipping sauce made from plums, vinegar, sugar, chillies and spices.

POLENTA also known as cornmeal; a flour-like cereal made of dried corn (maize). Also the dish made from it.

POMEGRANATE dark-red, leathery-skinned fresh fruit, about the size of an orange, filled with hundreds of seeds, each wrapped in an edible lucent-crimson pulp having a unique tangy sweet-sour flavour.

POMEGRANATE MOLASSES not to be confused with pomegranate syrup or grenadine (used in cocktails); pomegranate molasses is thicker, browner, and more concentrated in flavour – tart and sharp, slightly sweet and fruity.

POPPY SEEDS small, dried, bluish-grey seeds of the poppy plant, with a crunchy texture and a nutty flavour. Can be purchased whole or ground in delicatessens and most supermarkets.

PORK
belly fatty cut sold in rashers or in a piece, with or without rind or bone.
chinese barbecued roasted pork fillet with a sweet, sticky coating. Available from Asian food shops or specialty stores.
cutlets cut from ribs.
fillet skinless, boneless eye-fillet cut from the loin.
minced ground lean pork.
neck sometimes called pork scotch, boneless cut from the forelion.
shoulder joint sold with bone in or out.

RHUBARB a plant with long, green-red stalks; becomes sweet and edible when cooked.

RICER used to make the super-smooth potato called Paris mash. The potato goes into the container and, as the flat side is pressed down, it falls through the perforated base in fine, soft flakes.

ROCKET (ARUGULA) also called rugula and rucola; peppery green leaf eaten raw in salads or used in cooking. Baby rocket leaves are smaller and less peppery.

ROSEWATER extract made from crushed rose petals, called gulab in India; used for its aromatic quality in many sweetmeats and desserts.

SAGE pungent herb with narrow, grey-green leaves; slightly bitter with a slightly musty mint aroma.

SAKE Japan's favourite wine, made from fermented rice, is used for marinating, cooking and as part of dipping sauces. If sake is unavailable, dry sherry, vermouth or brandy can be substituted. If drinking sake, stand it first in a container in hot water for 20 minutes to warm it through.

SAMBAL OELEK also ulek or olek; an Indonesian salty paste made from ground chillies and vinegar.

SEAFOOD
fish fillet use your favourite firm-fleshed white fish fillet.
mussels should only be bought from a reliable fish market: they must be tightly closed when bought, indicating they are alive. Before cooking, scrub shells with a strong brush and remove the beards. Varieties include black and green-lip.
white fish means non-oily fish; includes bream, flathead, whiting, snapper, dhufish, redfish and ling.

SILVER BEET (SWISS CHARD) also known (incorrectly) as spinach; has fleshy stalks and large leaves, both of which can be prepared as for spinach.

SKEWERS metal or bamboo skewers can be used. Rub oil onto metal skewers to stop meat sticking; soak bamboo skewers in cold water for 1 hour to prevent them splintering or scorching during cooking.

SOUR CREAM *see cream*

SPINACH also known as english spinach and incorrectly, silver beet.

STAR ANISE a dried star-shaped pod whose seeds have an astringent aniseed flavour; commonly used to flavour stocks and marinades.

SUMAC a purple-red, astringent spice ground from berries growing on shrubs that flourish wild around the Mediterranean; adds a tart, lemony flavour to dips and dressings and goes well with barbecued meat. Can be found in Middle Eastern food stores.

TAHINI sesame seed paste available from Middle Eastern food stores and some supermarkets.

TAMARI similar to but thicker than japanese soy; very dark in colour with a distinctively mellow flavour. Good used as a dipping sauce or for basting.

TAMARIND the tamarind tree produces clusters of hairy brown pods, each of which is filled with seeds and a viscous pulp, that are dried and pressed into the blocks of tamarind found in Asian food shops. Gives a sweet-sour, slightly astringent taste to marinades, pastes, sauces and dressings.

THYME a member of the mint family; the "household" variety, simply called thyme in most shops, is French thyme; it has tiny grey-green leaves that give off a pungent minty, light-lemon aroma.

TREACLE thick, dark syrup not unlike molasses; a by-product of sugar refining.

TURMERIC also called kamin; is a rhizome related to galangal and ginger. Must be grated or pounded to release its acrid aroma and pungent flavour. Known for the golden colour it imparts, fresh turmeric can be substituted with the more commonly found dried powder.

V-SLICER cheaper and simpler to use than the Italian mandoline (but just as sharp), the V-slicer combines German efficiency and performance with its razor-sharp, flexible thin blades that slice, dice, shred and julienne.

VEAL
rack row of small chops or cutlets.
scaloppine a piece of lean steak hammered with a meat mallet until almost see-through; cook over high heat for as little time as possible.
schnitzel thinly sliced steak.

WALNUTS as well as being a good source of fibre and healthy oils, nuts contain a range of vitamins, minerals and other beneficial plant components called phytochemicals.

WATERCRESS one of the cress family, a large group of peppery greens used raw in salads, dips and sandwiches, or cooked in soups. Highly perishable, so it must be used as soon as possible after purchase.

WOMBOK (NAPA CABBAGE) also known as chinese or peking cabbage; elongated in shape with pale green, crinkly leaves, it is the most common cabbage in South-East Asia. Can be shredded or chopped and eaten raw or braised, steamed or stir-fried.

WORCESTERSHIRE SAUCE thin, dark-brown spicy sauce developed by the British when in India; used as a seasoning for meat, gravies and cocktails, and as a condiment.

YOGURT we use plain full-cream yogurt unless stated otherwise.
greek-style plain yogurt that has been strained in a cloth (traditionally muslin) to remove the whey and to give it a creamy consistency. It is ideal for use in dips and dressings.

ZA'ATAR a Middle Eastern herb and spice mixture which varies but always includes thyme (for which it gets its Arabic name), with ground sumac and, usually, toasted sesame seeds. It is sprinkled on yogurt and flatbreads and can be used as a rub on lamb or chicken to be grilled or roasted.

ZUCCHINI also called courgette; small, pale- or dark-green or yellow vegetable of the squash family. Harvested when young, its edible flowers can be stuffed with a mild cheese and deep-fried.

index

First published in 2012

ACP Books are published by ACP Magazines Limited,

a division of Nine Entertainment Co.

54 Park St, Sydney

GPO Box 4088, Sydney, NSW 2001.

phone (02) 9282 8618; fax (02) 9267 9438

acpbooks@acpmagazines.com.au; www.acpbooks.com.au

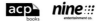

ACP BOOKS

Publishing Director, ACP Magazines · Gerry Reynolds

Publisher · Sally Wright

Editorial & Food Director · Pamela Clark

Creative Director · Hieu Chi Nguyen

Published and Distributed in the United Kingdom by Octopus Publishing Group

Endeavour House

189 Shaftesbury Avenue

London WC2H 8JY

United Kingdom

phone (+44)(0)207 632 5400; fax (+44)(0)207 632 5405

info@octopus-publishing.co.uk;

www.octopusbooks.co.uk

Printed by Toppan Printing Co, China

International foreign language rights, Brian Cearnes, ACP Books bcearnes@acpmagazines.com.au

A catalogue record for this book is available from the British Library.

ISBN 978-1-74245-346-0

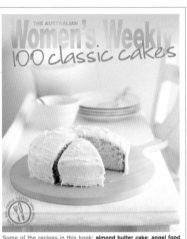

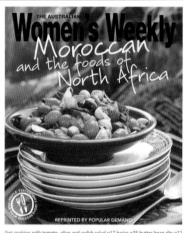

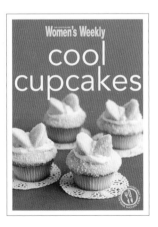